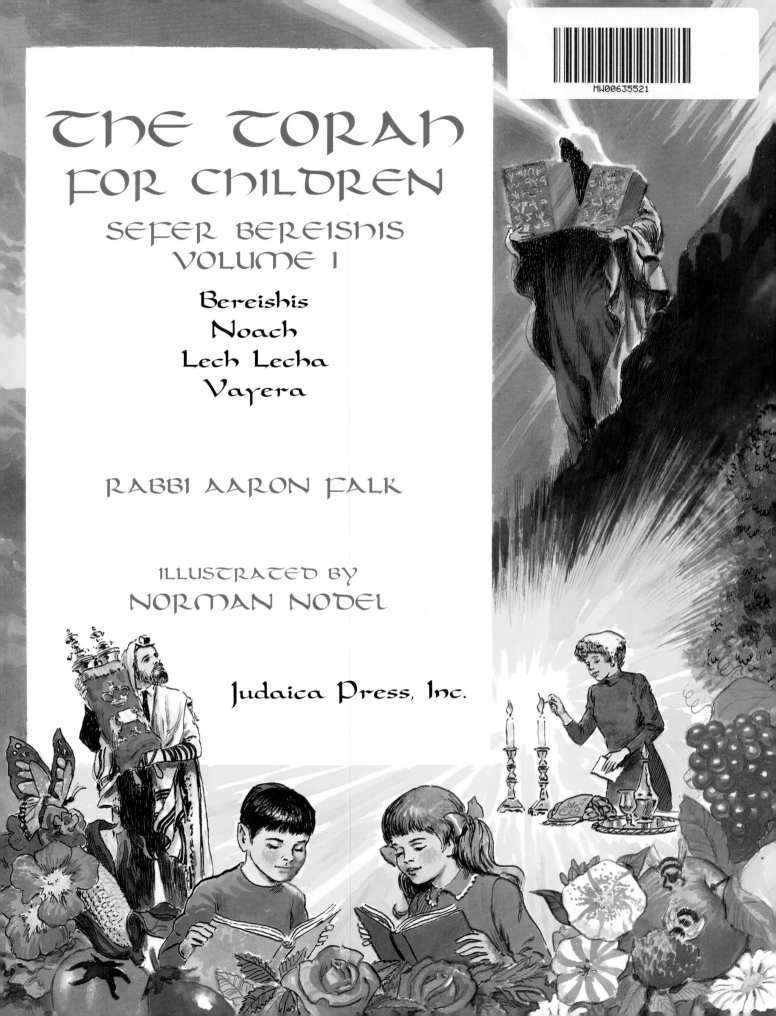

THE TORAH
FOR CHILDREN
SEFER BEREISHIS
VOLUME 1

Bereishis
Noach
Lech Lecha
Vayera

RABBI AARON FALK

ILLUSTRATED BY
NORMAN NODEL

Judaica Press, Inc.

Library of Congress Cataloging-in-Publication

Falk, Aaron.
    The Torah for children / by Aaron Falk : illustrated by Norman Nodel.
       p. cm.
    Contents: v. 1. Sefer Bereishis : Bereishis, Noach, Lech Lecha, Vayera.
    ISBN 1-880582-06-6, — ISBN 1-880582-07-4 (pbk.)
    1. Bible stories, English—O.T. Pentateuch.   [1. Bible stories—O.T.]
I. Nodel, Norman, ill.   II. Title.
BS551.2.F26   1993   92-28623
221.9'505—dc20   CIP

© Copyright 1993

The Judaica Press, Inc.

New York, NY

Translated by Tehila Beckerman

from the Hebrew

דפתעות לפרשיות השבוע/כרך א

Adapted from the Translation

by Rachel J. Witty

Library of Congress Catalog Card Number 92-28623

ISBN 1-880582-06-6 (hardcover)

ISBN 1-880582-07-4 (softcover)

הרב לוי יצחק הלוי הורוויץ

דער באסטאנער רבי

Grand Rabbi Levi Y. Horowitz

מוסדות בוסטון בארה"ק
בנשיאות האדמו"ר שליט"א
מעלות האדמו"ר מבוסטון ז
הר נוף, ירושלים Israel

ב"ה

כ"ז סיון, תשנ"ג

The book "Torah for Children" is beautifully illustrated and catches both the eye and the heart of the child. It is needless to say that we must do everything in our power to instill a love of Torah in our children, and every Bais Medrash makes a new contribution to the study of our heritage.

I have heard that when children see these pages they become motivated to learn and delve into the Torah.

I therefore would like to extend my blessings to the author, Rabbi Aaron Falk and to Judaica Press for publishing this work. May they make a great contribution to promoting the love of Torah.

המצפה לישועת השם
ולהרמת קרן ישראל

The Bostoner Rebbe
Har Nof, Jerusalem

IN THE BEGINNING, THERE WA

OTHING BUT GOD.

BEREISHIS

בראשית

THE FIRST DAY OF CREATION

On the first day, Hashem (God) created the light.
He separated the light from the darkness
and made the day and the night.

Why? For whom?

THE SECOND DAY OF CREATION

On the second day, Hashem finished the sky
and separated the waters of the heavens
from the waters of the earth.

But there was no living thing to enjoy the light or the sky.
Why did Hashem create them?

THE THIRD DAY OF CREATION

On the third day, Hashem made the land appear
and formed the seas.
He brought out plants and their seeds,
fruit trees and their seeds.

But there was still no one to enjoy all these wonderful things.

BEREISHIS
בראשית

THE FOURTH DAY OF CREATION

On the fourth day, Hashem created the shining stars,
the warming sun, and the moon, which gives us light at night.

Yet there was still no one to look at them.
So why were they created? And for whom?

THE FIFTH DAY OF CREATION

On the fifth day, Hashem created
the fish and the birds.

Perhaps Hashem prepared everything for them.
No, Hashem did not create the world for them.
Then for whom?

THE SIXTH DAY OF CREATION

On the sixth day, Hashem created all the animals.
But not even for the animals did Hashem create the world.

After everything else in the world was created,
Hashem created the first man, Adam.
Hashem gave Adam a very special gift—
a wife named Chavah (Eve).

All the wonderful things that Hashem had created
were for Adam and Chavah.

BEREISHIS
בראשית

THE SEVENTH DAY OF CREATION

On the seventh day, Hashem rested,
and it was Shabbos.

Shabbos reminds us that Hashem
created this wonderful world for us
to observe the commandments, *mitzvos*,
and to perform good deeds, *maasim tovim*.

6

THANKING HASHEM

Adam was created in the image of Hashem.
Hashem created Adam's body out of the dust of the earth.

This teaches us not to be too proud.

Hashem also gave Adam a holy soul, a *neshamah*.
Therefore, we should do good and holy deeds.

Hashem is always helping us, but sometimes we forget this.
How do we thank Hashem?
We thank Him by obeying His commandments
and performing good deeds.

BEREISHIS
בראשית

THE TREE OF KNOWLEDGE

Hashem made a beautiful garden, *gan eden,*
where Adam and Chavah could have a good and happy life.
Hashem allowed them to eat fruit from all the trees—
except for the Tree of Knowledge, the *etz hadaas.*

But Chavah listened to the snake,
who told her to eat the fruit from the Tree of Knowledge.
She gave it to Adam, and he ate it, too.

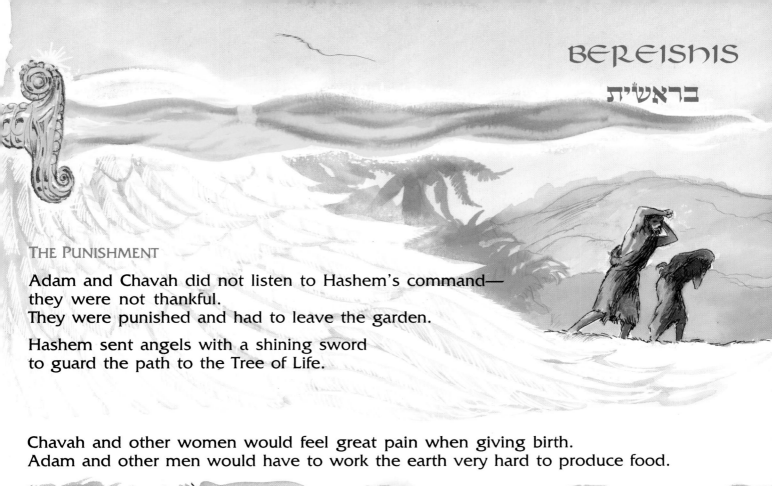

The Punishment

Adam and Chavah did not listen to Hashem's command—
they were not thankful.
They were punished and had to leave the garden.

Hashem sent angels with a shining sword
to guard the path to the Tree of Life.

Chavah and other women would feel great pain when giving birth.
Adam and other men would have to work the earth very hard to produce food.

The snake, who told them to sin, was also punished.
All snakes would forevermore crawl on the ground
and eat the dust of the earth.

9

BEREISHIS
בראשית

THE BROTHERS

Adam and Chavah had two sons,
Kayin (Cain) and Hevel (Abel).
Kayin was a farmer and Hevel was a shepherd.
The brothers wanted to thank Hashem,
so they each brought Him gift-offerings.

Hashem liked Hevel's offering better than Kayin's.
Kayin was so jealous of his brother that he killed him.

When Hashem asked Kayin where Hevel was,
Kayin replied, "I do not know.
Am I my brother's keeper—*hashomer achi anochi*?"

But Hashem knew what Kayin had done.
As a punishment Kayin had to wander the earth.

It is so sad that Kayin's jealousy
overcame his love for his brother.

Adam and Chavah had a third son, and they named him Sheis (Seth).

NOACH

נח

THE DESTRUCTION OF THE WORLD

Noach (Noah) was a righteous man, a *tzaddik*.
The other people of his time were wicked.
Hashem told Noach to build an ark, a *taiva*, made of gopher wood
because He was going to bring a flood to destroy all life.

11

Hashem told Noach to bring every kind
of animal, bird, reptile, and insect into the ark.

He told Noach to take seven pairs—
male and female—of each kosher one,
and one pair of each of the others.

NOACH

THE FLOOD

It started to rain.

Noach, his three sons,
his wife, and their wives
all went into the ark.

It rained and rained for forty days and forty nights
until water covered the entire earth.
Only Noach and all those in the ark
were saved from the flood.

The wicked people were not saved.

NOACH
נֹחַ

NOACH

נח

Long after the rain had stopped,
Noach sent out a raven to look for dry land.
The raven came back to the ark.

Noach sent out a dove, but it also returned.

Noach waited a week and sent out the dove again.
The dove returned carrying an olive leaf in its beak.

When Noach sent out the dove yet again,
it did not return to the ark at all.
Noach realized that the dove had found dry land.

REBUILDING THE WORLD

Everyone came out of the ark.
They saw that wickedness had destroyed the world.
Noach understood that they would have to rebuild
a new world of good deeds.

So Noach built an altar, a *mizbaiach*,
and brought a sacrifice of kosher animals and birds to Hashem.

Hashem made a rainbow in the sky,
as a sign that He would never again bring
such a flood upon the world.

17

NOACह

THE TOWER

The people who lived in Shinar
thought they were very clever.
They started to build a powerful city
and, in it, a tower to reach up to the sky.

They thought that when the tower was finished,
they would be so powerful and smart
that they would not need any help from Hashem.

Hashem showed them they were not so smart.
He mixed up their language so they did not understand each other
and could no longer build the tower.
They were scattered all over the world.

The place where they were building the tower was called Bavel,
from the Hebrew word *balal,* which means to mix up.
This reminds us that we always need Hashem,
even when we think we are smart.

18

LECH LECHA

לך לך

AVRAM AND SARAI

In the days of Avram and his wife Sarai,
people bowed and prayed to idols.
But Avram and Sarai worshipped only One God, Hashem.

When Avram was seventy-five years old,
Hashem told him to go to *Eretz Canaan,* Israel.
Avram loved Hashem and followed His command.
There was a famine there, so Avram moved to Egypt.

Even when Sarai was taken from Avram
to be a wife to Pharoah, the ruler of Egypt,
Avram continued to believe in Hashem.
Pharoah was punished, and Sarai was unharmed.

Avram and Sarai proved by their love of Hashem
that they were worthy of being the first Jews.

Avram bravely rescued his nephew Lot
from the four kings who held him captive,
even though Lot had left Avram
after their shepherds had quarelled.

THE PROMISES OF HASHEM

Hashem made promises to Avram in the *Bris Bein Habesarim*, the Covenant Between the Pieces.

Hashem promised to give the Land of Canaan
to Avram and his descendants,
who would be as numerous as the stars in the sky.

Hashem also told Avram that his descendants
would one day be slaves in a strange land,
go out with great wealth, and return to *Eretz Canaan*.

Avram and his maidservant, Hagar,
were blessed with a son, Yishmael (Ishmael),
but he was wild and unruly.

20

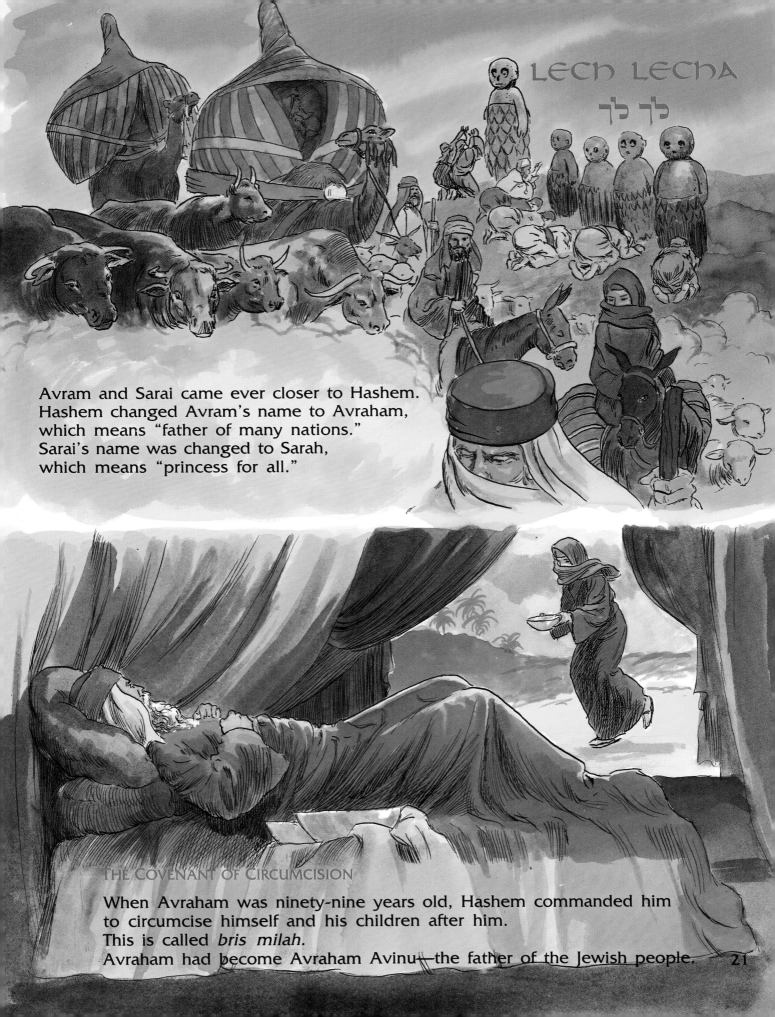

LECH LECHA
לך לך

Avram and Sarai came ever closer to Hashem.
Hashem changed Avram's name to Avraham,
which means "father of many nations."
Sarai's name was changed to Sarah,
which means "princess for all."

THE COVENANT OF CIRCUMCISION

When Avraham was ninety-nine years old, Hashem commanded him
to circumcise himself and his children after him.
This is called *bris milah.*
Avraham had become Avraham Avinu—the father of the Jewish people.

21

VAYERA

וירא

HACHNOSAS ORCHIM: HOSPITALITY

Avraham's *bris milah* caused him great pain.
He was old and it took time to heal.
Suddenly Avraham saw three wanderers.
Even though he was weak, he ran to invite them in.

He brought them water to wash.
He asked Sarah to make them some cakes.
Avraham hurried to bring a calf and prepared
a delicious feast for his guests.

The three guests—who were really angels sent by Hashem—
blessed Avraham and Sarah, saying they would have a son.

THE BIRTH OF YITZCHAK

Sarah thought she was too old to have a baby, so she laughed.
Avraham knew that Hashem could do anything.
A year later, Sarah gave birth to Yitzchak.

VAYERA

וירא

The people in Sodom were very wicked,
but Lot had settled there, thinking he could become rich.

24

VAYERA
וירא

THE DESTRUCTION OF SODOM

Hashem told Avraham that He would destroy Sodom
and its wicked people.
Avraham prayed to Hashem
and pleaded with Him to save the people.

That evening, two *malachim,* angels, arrived in Sodom.
The wicked people threatened them.
They did not know that the visitors
were *malachim* sent by Hashem.

Lot protected them from the mob.
The *malachim* warned Lot to leave the city
because Hashem was going to destroy Sodom.

Lot, his wife, and his two daughters fled from Sodom.
The *malachim* warned them not to look back,
but Lot's wife looked back and was turned into a pillar of salt.
Only Lot and his daughters escaped.

Despite Avraham's prayers, Hashem destroyed the city
because the people were so wicked,
and there were no *tzadikkim,* righteous people, among them.

25

VAYERA

וירא

AKEIDAS YITZCHAK: THE BINDING OF YITZCHAK

In Avraham's time, people showed their love
for their idols by sacrificing their children to them.
The Torah teaches us to show our love for Hashem
by caring for and teaching our children.

Once though, Hashem tested Avraham by asking him
to bring Yitzchak to the altar as a sacrifice.
Would kind Avraham,
who had waited so long for Yitzchak,
be able to do such a frightening thing?

For three days Avraham and his son traveled to a faraway place.
There Avraham's love and fear of Hashem would be tested.

Avraham prepared Yitzchak as a sacrifice,
just as Hashem had commanded.
He took the knife, but an angel of Hashem stopped Avraham,
warning him not to harm Yitzchak in any way.

VAYERA
וירא

By following Hashem's command
to place Yitzchak on the altar
as a sacrifice,
Avraham had shown his love
and fear of Hashem.

Hashem did not command Avraham to sacrifice Yitzchak.
In the thicket, Hashem revealed a ram to Avraham,
and Avraham sacrificed it instead.

Hashem never commanded and never will command
a father to sacrifice his child.